Working Animals

Acting Animals

by Julie Murray

Dash!
LEVELED READERS
An Imprint of Abdo Zoom • abdobooks.com

2

Dash!
LEVELED READERS

Level 1 – Beginning
Short and simple sentences with familiar words or patterns for children who are beginning to understand how letters and sounds go together.

Level 2 – Emerging
Longer words and sentences with more complex language patterns for readers who are practicing common words and letter sounds.

Level 3 – Transitional
More developed language and vocabulary for readers who are becoming more independent.

THIS BOOK CONTAINS RECYCLED MATERIALS

abdobooks.com

Published by Abdo Zoom, a division of ABDO, PO Box 398166, Minneapolis, Minnesota 55439.
Copyright © 2020 by Abdo Consulting Group, Inc. International copyrights reserved in all countries.
No part of this book may be reproduced in any form without written permission from the publisher.
Dash!™ is a trademark and logo of Abdo Zoom.

Printed in the United States of America, North Mankato, Minnesota.
052019
092019

Photo Credits: Alamy, Everette Collection, Getty Images, iStock
Production Contributors: Kenny Abdo, Jennie Forsberg, Grace Hansen, John Hansen
Design Contributors: Dorothy Toth, Neil Klinepier

Library of Congress Control Number: 2018963313

Publisher's Cataloging in Publication Data

Names: Murray, Julie, author.
Title: Acting animals / by Julie Murray.
Description: Minneapolis, Minnesota : Abdo Zoom, 2020 | Series: Working animals | Includes online resources and index.
Identifiers: ISBN 9781532127304 (lib. bdg.) | ISBN 9781532128288 (ebook) | ISBN 9781532128776 (Read-to-me ebook)
Subjects: LCSH: Working animals--Juvenile literature. | Animals as actors--Juvenile literature. | Animals in motion pictures--Juvenile literature. | Animals on television--Juvenile literature.
Classification: DDC 791.43--dc23

Table of
Contents

Acting Animals

Crystal is a monkey. She is also an acting animal! She has been in more than 20 movies and TV shows.

Many different kinds of
animals can be actors.
Dogs, horses, and bears
are just a few.

Some animals act in movies. Others are in **commercials**. Some might perform at a zoo.

Bamboo Harvester was an acting animal. He played a talking horse on the 1960s TV show *Mister Ed*.

Moose was a Jack Russell Terrier. He was in the movie *My Dog Skip*. He was also on the TV show *Frasier*.

Training

It is hard work becoming an animal actor. A **trainer** works with the animal. They teach them new skills or tricks. This can take months or even years.

The animal needs to be comfortable with its **trainer**. They form a special **bond**.

Acting animals need to be smart. They have to follow **commands** while working.

Many acting animals get paid. They make money for their special skills or talents.

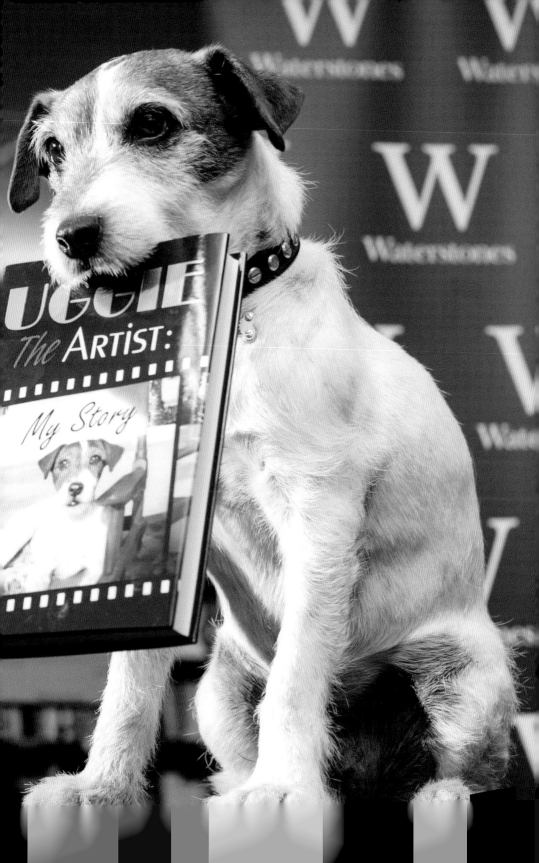

More Facts

- Dogs, ducks, and zebras have walked the red carpet!

- Live animal shows can be dangerous. Roy Horn was attacked by his lion. It happened during a live show in Las Vegas. He was badly hurt.

- The American Humane Association protects acting animals. They make sure the animals are treated well.

Glossary

bond – a feeling that brings people and animals together.

command – to lead and control.

commercial – an advertisement on television.

trainer – a person who trains animals to prepare them for a job, activity, or sport.

Index

Online Resources

Booklinks
NONFICTION NETWORK
FREE! ONLINE NONFICTION RESOURCES

To learn more about acting animals, please visit **abdobooklinks.com** or scan this QR code. These links are routinely monitored and updated to provide the most current information available.